MAY I HAVE AN ALPHABET FOR JUST ONE DAY?

COLORING BOOK

Copyright © 2009
by Barbara " Muffin" Pierce 63198-Pier
ISBN: Softcover 978-0-9840260-2-9

All rights reserved. No part of this book may be reproduced or transmitted in any form by any means, electronic or mechanical, including photocopying, recording, or by any information storage or retrieval system, without permission in writing from the copyright owner.

This is a work of fiction. Names, characters, places and incidents either are the product of the author's imagination or are used fictiously, and any resemblance to any actual persons, living or dead, events, or locales is entirely coincidental.

This book was printed in the United States of America

To order additional copies of this book, contact:
Unique Euphony Publishing Group
(706) 577-3197
www.uniqueeuphony.com
inquiries@uniqueeuphony.com

Mrs. Stewart is my teacher. She asked me to bring all of the alphabets to school tomorrow, but I don't have any to bring. I know I am going to ask my friend **A**lex to let me use his letter **A** from his name **A**lex. If he says its okay, then his name will be "lex" for just one day, and what a funny name to say.

I'll call my friend **B**rianna; maybe she will let me use the letter **B** from her name **B**rianna. If she says its okay, then her name will be "rianna" for just one day, which is not a bad new name to say.

I have to find the letter **C**. I will go and find my friend **C**oby. I know she will let me use the letter **C**, although her name will be "oby" oh boy! That sounds silly, but it's just for one day, I think that's okay.

I will ask my friend **D**alyn, or my other friend **D**earius who sometimes we call "Big Boy". I bet I could get at least one **D**, because all I need is one, which one will it be, **D**earius or **D**alyn? **Umm**… let's see!

I will ask my brother Eddie to let me use his letter **E** from his name **E**ddie. I call **E**ddie my little brother anyway. So to miss an **E** from his name for just one day, my little brother will be okay.

I know my friend **F**ranklin will let me use the letter **F**, from his name **F**ranklin, because he is so… friendly. I know it will be okay for just one day.

Garrett is one great guy, so I know he will let me use the letter **G** from his name Garrett for just one day.

Jaylen will help me with the letter **J**, although we will have to call her "aylen," but I think that will be okay for just one day.

I will ask my little cousin **K**irk to help me with the letter **K**. I know he will help me by letting me use the letter **K** from his name **K**irk for just one day. Hey! He has two **K**'s in his name **K**irk, but only one for a day will be okay.

Lenny lives in my neighborhood. I always let him play with my toys. I am sure he will let me use his letter **L** from his name **L**enny. Then his name will be "enny," but I think that will be okay for just one day.

One day **M**arilyn may be my girlfriend, but I don't know if she will let me use her letter **M**. I am going to ask her anyway if I could use her **M** for just one day.

My best friend **N**efertari will help me with the letter **N**. Her name will be "efertari," what a weird name for just one day, but because she is my best friend, I know she will let me use the letter **N** anyway for just one day, Okay?

NEFERTARI

Where in the world am I going to find **O**, **P**, **Q** and **R**? I do not think I have any friends that could help me find such alphabets, but I think Mr. Alpha at the candy store will let me use the **O**, **P**, **Q**, and **R**. There has to be some candy with the alphabets **O**, **P**, **Q** and **R**. I am on my way to the candy store to ask Mr.Alpha, may I have these alphabets for just one day. I hope it will be okay?

OPQR CANDY STORE

I should ask my teacher Mrs. Stewart for the letter **S**, but I have to have the letter **S** when I go to school tomorrow, so I have to ask someone else. I know… I will ask my neighbor Mrs. Sherman to please let me use the **S** from her name **S**herman. If she says it is okay, then her name will be Mrs. "herman," and I am sure that will be okay for just one day.

I think my grandpa could help me with the letter **T**, but I have to wait until he comes home from his church meeting. Grandpa has plenty of friends that he could ask like the twins, Mr. **T**ony, or Mr. **T**im. All I need is a **T** for just one day, please?

Of course I will use the **U** from my own name **U**lysses. I want to thank you mom and dad for giving me the name **U**lysses. I can keep that letter **U** for more than a day, Hooray! Hooray! I am **U**lysses for more than one day!

My big sister **V**al will let me use her **V** from her name **V**alencia. But for one day her name will be "alencia." I will not be able to call her **V**al, but I think I like the name "alencia" anyway, for just one day.

My Uncle **W**illiam will let me use his letter **W** from his name **W**illiam. He loves to help me with my school work. I will call him uncle for just one day, and I am sure that will be okay.

Umm…**X**avier, I have two friends with the name **X**avier. Which one will it be? All I need is one **X**. They are both my friends, and they are both **X**aviers, but I don't think it matters, so I will ask one of them if I could use the letter **X** for just one day. I am sure between th two of them it will be okay.

I do not have to worry about the letter **Y**, because my cousin who lives next door will let me use the letter **Y** from her name **Y**asmine. I am sure she could do without a **Y** for just one day. Why, because she is my cousin, and we share almost anything. Say, I think I'll call her "asmine" for just one day. I think that will be okay.

I will ask my twin brother and sister, **Z**achary or **Z**ykeria to let me use the letter **Z** from their names. My twin brother and sister could do without a **Z** for just one day, because our family and friends call them Little Keke, and Baby Keria for nicknames anyway.

Because of all my family, and friends that can do without their alphabets for just one day, I have all of my alphabets at school today. Oh boy... that's great! I have all my alphabets for just one day.

www.ingramcontent.com/pod-product-compliance
Lightning Source LLC
Chambersburg PA
CBHW051215290426
44109CB00021B/2466